THE BLACK SWAN MARKET

Now Containing Also the New Science Manifesto!

THE BLACK SWAN MARKET, NATHAN COPPEDGE

© 2022 Nathan Coppedge. The New Science Manifesto was previously publicly-released.

THE BLACK SWAN MARKET

By Nathan Coppedge

THE BLACK SWAN MARKET, NATHAN COPPEDGE

,,,

CHAPTER 1: A PREVIEW OF THE IMPORTANCE OF SWANS

Something is interesting. Maybe it is historical development. Maybe it is money. Maybe it is logical truths. Maybe it is urbanization, or modern commercial markets.

Some have identified this nuancée with the Pharmakon, the idea of tradeoffs which define generational cultural shifts. Others have defined the difference in terms of supercultural zeits, modulations of the unconscious collective mind, or in terms of Taleb's concept of the black swan, or one of its many variations such as welfare economics or other cultural or policy shifts.

Features of the landscape which fascinate us include general forms such as computational complexity, individual performance variations like IQ and success, situational factors, and numerous aspects of markets, products, people, animals, environments, climates, general cognitive patterns, and almost anything else.

What these factors or variables hold in common, ideally, is that they are interesting, and what makes things interesting economically is this 'explanatory factor' analogous to a black swan.

The unpredictability, or sometimes predictability of markets makes black swans fascinating, and uniquely so. And this is even true if we generalize 'swans' to mean something more nebulous and include multiple definitions of 'swan'.

To me, all these other types: white swan, grey swan, black swan (concepts introduced at some point since Taleb's book to describe market patterns)—are all the same idea.

They are attempts—successful, relatively speaking—to describe patterns in markets which include particular market-specific traits, traits which are exciting.

Most exciting of all market traits is the black swan, because it describes a case which is exponentially irregular, and exponentially irreducible. The traits of a black swan become, directly, in a kind of ideal way, the properties of a market. The ideal black swan is not just a market event, it is a market reality.

By studying the nature and importance of 'swan events', the powerful apparition of economics becomes powerfully apparent as a real-factor not just a simple-factor of this kind of computational archeology.

That is just a preview of this hidden nature which black swans and golden ages entail.

It has been shown recently in my work that golden ages have followed a particular path of inheritance from the Chinese concept of the dead ancestor and the venerated family member.

GOLDEN AGE SUPERSTRATEGY

ANCIENT TIMES

VEN OF GHOSTS   VEN OF FAMILY

GOLDEN AGES

GLOR IN ABSTRACT   GLOR OF MATERIALS

BLACK SWANS

EXP KNOWLEDGE   EXP MECHANICS

REPRODUCIBLE UNDER NATHAN COPPEDGE

Within Europe, Chinese knowledge was regarded with suspicion, and the concepts were treated as superstitions which had the power of philosophy. Religions converted the same dichotomy in the West into a division between the abstract and the material.

Finally, I suggest, this same current manifests directly into the traits of black swans.

Abstraction en purum conferred directly into exponentially-efficient knowledge, and physics conferred into exponentially-efficient mechanics.

It is easy to see that these two divisions of exponential efficiency are things on which all human life depends.

Survival in the universal environment depends on understanding the universe, which requires exceptional understanding. The method to reach exceptional understanding is through computers, using processes which must beat one another. The most superior such process would achieve exponential efficiency in order to have technical advantages on other forms of knowledge.

Secondly, we can see that exponentially-efficient mechanics is also necessary for human survival.

Exponentially-efficient mechanics is necessary if we are to have technological superiority on our environment. It is a natural development of the so-called rational conquest of nature. The alternative to exponentially-efficient mechanics is Anarchic dissolution into our previous natures.

CHAPTER 2: BEFORE APPLICATIONS

This year I was asked to answer a question regarding whether humans would live to 500 years.

I answered that the resolution might involve what are called 'black swan markets'.

As I am writing this, the concept is still in development, it is very new.

The most basic and for now useful formulation is that it involves the following:

- Black swans, with the structure previously given:
    - Exponentially-efficient knowledge (objective knowledge).
    - Exponentially-efficient mechanics (perpetual motion machines).
- A context-of black swans, in other words, their materialization in dimensional space.
    - The existence of processes engaged with black swans.
    - A process immersed in black swans.
- Other factors could also come into play due to the dynamic nature of black swans, for example, immediately:
    - The concept of applied knowledge, for example, the Applied Theory of Anything.

- The concept of applied perpetual motion, for example, many new inventions such as self-powered objects and enhanced performance devices.

Part of the thing to understand about these 'superior factors' or 'exponentive variables' is that they are black swans in their most general form. They are even black swans reduced to a kind of concise predictability.

Since these are concerned with the two traditional halves of a golden age, it may be unlikely that a more comprehensive theory of predictability would occur without further inheritance.

Meanwhile, the most direct line to inheriting these concepts is simply to apply them to practical fields.

This could mean most likely that these super-factors, minus the applications embody the fullest extent of coherence within the over-arching field of black swans. This also further implicates that in some way both perpetual motion and objective knowledge are coherent, an insight I APPLIED to reach a Theory of Anything, also known (currently to very few) as the Results Theorem.

If we view the **THEORY OF ANYTHING (YES, THE REAL THEORY OF ANYTHING) as an APPLICATION... OF... BLACK SWANS...**

THEN… We get an idea of what I mean by BLACK SWAN MARKETS.

Soon we will get further into the phenomenology of this new paradigm, a paradigm which is hopefully emerging in the next 1000 years + / - and which may involve itself in the extreme with the concept of Evolution Praecox, and pretty much any other legitimately big idea you might imagine, including immortality.

CHAPTER 3: BLACK SWAN PARADIGMS

I am not trying to imply that black swan markets are the only type of paradigm.

Indeed, more traditional black swans (and let us be clear, my concepts are certainly radical, at least as of now) are still profound.

We can observe some market impacts with what I call traditional swans: for example, we can observe a trend towards exponential improvement in the whole market. Exponential Efficiency would treat this modularly.

We can also observe that the traditional black swan economy has a dimensional impact. That is, it has specifications and variables which are hypothetically useful. This 'latent economy' understands itself enough to foresee some improvements when it is given enough privilege. The traditional black swan allows the law of identity to occasionally make renovations and infrastructure improvements.

The nouveau black swan though would by comparison be hyper-dimensional. It would create what I call 'magical infrastructure': systems that pay for themselves. Resource innovations and process improvements beyond the traditional meaning of economics. It would create what might be called 'free markets' using a new meaning similar to 'free-energy markets' rather than the more-traditional 'free-will markets'.

All the factors of traditional black swans would still be present: there is emphasis on dimensions and economic excitement. There is emphasis on exponential development and technological improvement. But now, with the abstract and material structural improvement implied by exponential efficiency, there would be a further compounding of all significant potentials 'at the planck length' so to speak, by macro-economic standards. The economy would have inherent growth, and inherent potential. It would be what I call 'an investment economy'. An economy that has 'free banks' and 'exponential investments'.

It would be the foundation for what are known in the future as 'green banks' and 'free investment entrepreneering'.

If the traditional-swan is the paradigm of human ecology, the nouveau swan is the paradigm of human econometry.

CHAPTER 4: REALIZING THE POTENTIAL OF THE T.O.E.

To be more conservative, let's consider only the abstract.

Let's say hypothetically you have a formula which predicts just about anything. It can be used to find new research applications, it can be used to understand outer-space, or communicate with aliens, or even improve the performance of a computer. It can do pretty much anything you want it to do.

Such a thing is obviously useful. The concept of exponential efficiency defines the furthest boundary of what usefulness could ever mean.

Now imagine you have something as practical as the Theory of Anything except it involves a physical machine.

If you got a little mental orgasm there, that is what I am aiming for.

Exponential efficiency is a profound idea that can even apply to mechanics.

But I won't say it applies to an unlimited number of things, because exponential efficiency as I have said, is currently implicated in only two fields: the two halves of black swans.

Fortunately, black swans are very interesting.

CHAPTER 5: REAL PERPETUAL MOTION

Picture a machine that moves forever through exponential efficiency. Would you consider at first that such a thing is possible?

Consider the principle of dividing unity by fractions. We can observe that even though both numbers are less than one, and the process is usually conservative, the end product is actually a greater number. It can be illustrated with this diagram:

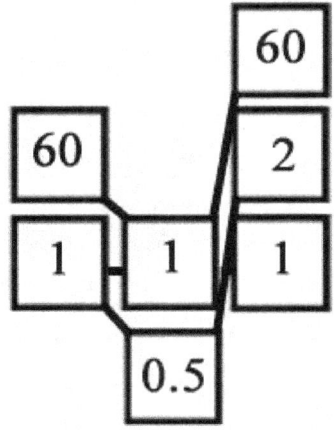

Is the process of calculating efficiency really so strict and universal that it would exclude a conservative process in creating an un-conservative result? Wouldn't that result just be less conservative? By this reasoning we can conclude some hyper-efficient processes probably exist in nature by sheer mathematical probability.

Now, imagine that you have a structured process analogous to a computer. Wouldn't this process, normally acting conservatively on larger numbers, sometimes apply to fractions?

Recently, in the last few years, I came up with a general formula for efficiency, which I think physicists would agree with, at least in simple cases (this is to give a rough estimate relative to unity):

FOR ORDINARY OBJECTS

[(MIN EFF + 1) - (MAX EFF + 1)] / [0.5 (MIN EFF + MAX EFF)]

Only, it has a loophole. When the Max Efficiency is divided by two, which would normally be conservative, in this formula, since it is properly subtracted from the lower efficiency, the end result is actually over-unity:

FOR PERPETUAL MOTION:

$[(\text{MIN EFF} + 1) - ((\text{MAX EFF} / 2) + 1)] / [0.5 (\text{MIN EFF} + \text{MAX EFF})]$

A typical result for this equation is < 150%, it is not very extreme, but it is still interesting.

That by itself is a black swan.

Now if we get to applied black swans, we can see that if we add lighter-than-air properties we could get perpetual motion machines that are lighter than air and self-powered, as shown below:

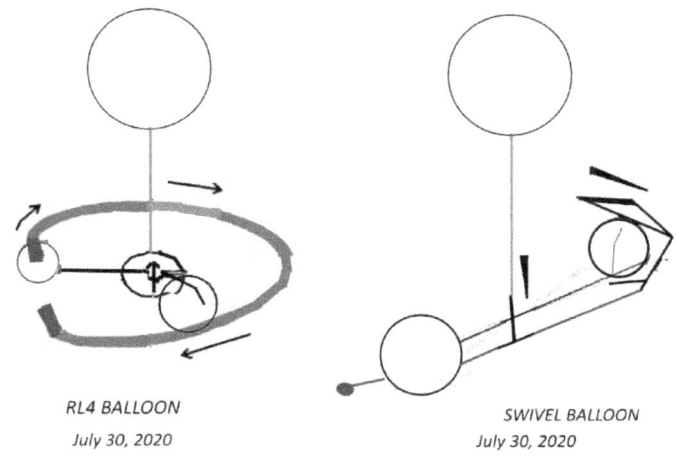

REAL PERPETUAL MOTION FLYING MACHINES 2nd Generation

RL4 BALLOON
July 30, 2020

SWIVEL BALLOON
July 30, 2020

NATHAN COPPEDGE

The principle of exponential efficiency says that the properties held between a flying machine and a standard working perpetual motion machine are the same, except that the flying machine operates UPSIDE DOWN, and the weight of the lever contributes to the buoyancy on the shorter end.

Using principles similar to these we can also construct a wide variety of different devices, if we have sufficient skill. Some of them are shown on the following pages:

1st FULLY PROVABLE

WHAT I CALL THE "1ST FULLY PROVABLE PERPETUAL MOTION MACHINE"
[MODIFIED FOR GREATER WORKABILITY] DIAGRAM WITH STATS BY
FEB 14, 2021

9 degree angle is about 58.25 application. Max lvg is 2.24, Min is 1.73.
Min HvyMass = Max Lvg X 0.5825 + 1 = 2.3 mass units, (first check if able to lift ball to max leverage)
Max HvyMass = Min Lvg + 1 = 2.73 mass units, (check if still able to lift ball at min leverage)
Then there is a window of nearly 0.43 the mass of the marble
to account for friction! In a balance! So, it works!

weight ratio: as one quarter,
one penny 1 marble and 5
in of duct tape is to 1 marble
lever ratio 10.8 - 14 : 6.25
track angle ~0.5deg
upwards-sloped
lever angle
est 2 - 9 deg
downwards-sloped.

NOTE: NEW LIP TO
DIRECT FREE-FALL
MAY BE IMPORTANT

STEP 1: BALL HAS ALTITUDE TO APPLY PRESSURE TO FIRST MODULAR COUNTER-WEIGHTED LEVER. (B.1)

WORKING RATIOS in straight lever experiment.

STEP 2: BALL RISES ALONG INCLINE, HELPED BY FIXED TRACK SUPPORT A1. UNTIL IT REACHES BEGINNING OF 2ND MODULAR LEVER. (B.2)
STEP 3: BALL WEIGHT HAS SUFFICIENT HEIGHT TO ACTIVATE LEVER AT SAME INITIAL HEIGHT, IN SPITE OF ITS LOWER BASE HEIGHT. PMM!

UPRIGHT PERPETUAL MOTION

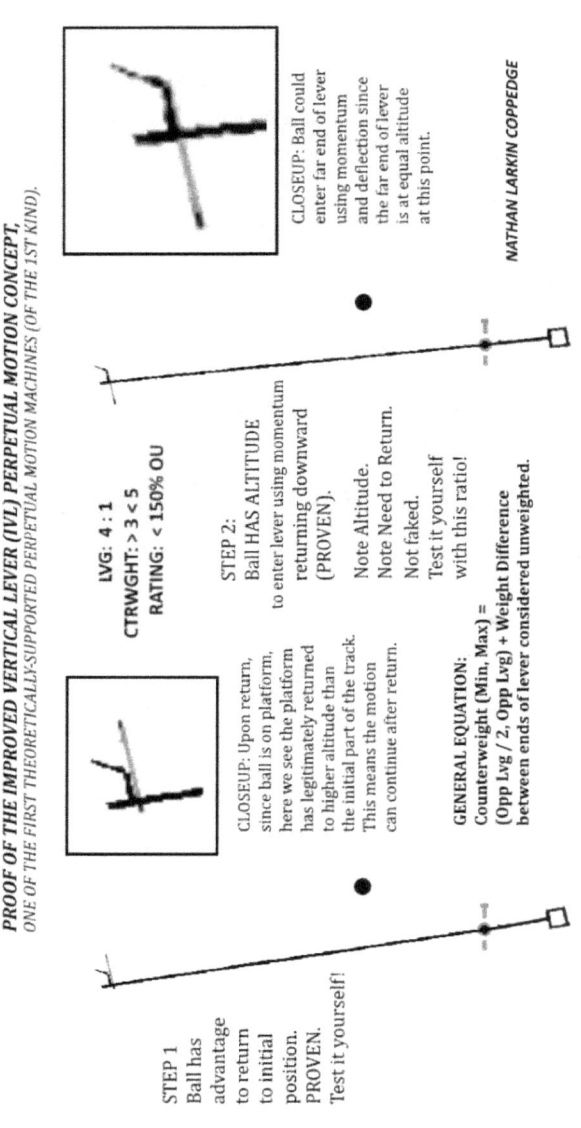

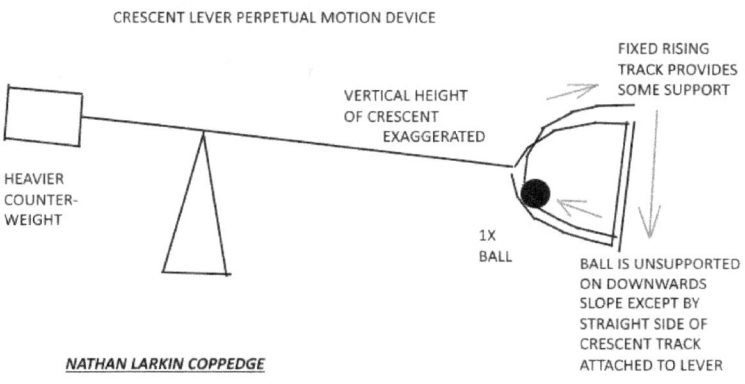

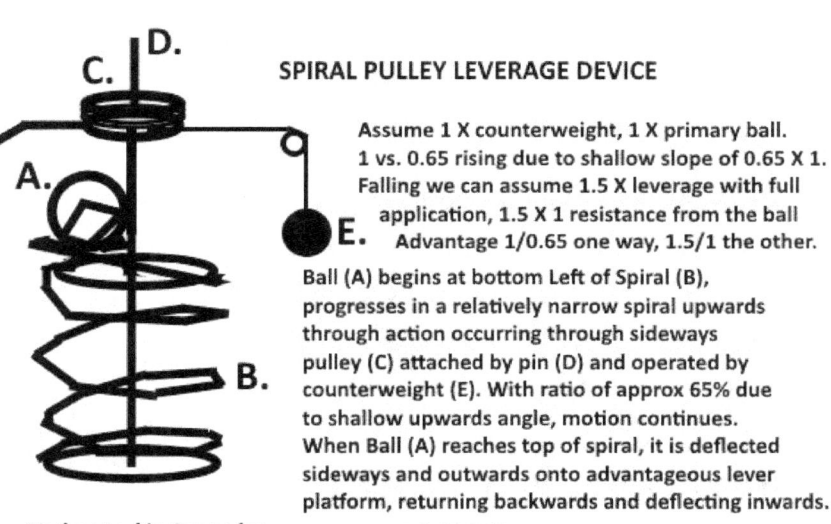

SPIRAL PULLEY LEVERAGE DEVICE

Assume 1 X counterweight, 1 X primary ball. 1 vs. 0.65 rising due to shallow slope of 0.65 X 1. Falling we can assume 1.5 X leverage with full application, 1.5 X 1 resistance from the ball Advantage 1/0.65 one way, 1.5/1 the other.

Ball (A) begins at bottom Left of Spiral (B), progresses in a relatively narrow spiral upwards through action occurring through sideways pulley (C) attached by pin (D) and operated by counterweight (E). With ratio of approx 65% due to shallow upwards angle, motion continues. When Ball (A) reaches top of spiral, it is deflected sideways and outwards onto advantageous lever platform, returning backwards and deflecting inwards.

Nathan Larkin Coppedge   July 18, 2021

CHAPTER 6: PERPETUAL MOTION PARADIGMS

Obviously at this point, perpetual motion is something which does not just require a designer, as many would think.

It also requires a builder. For this reason, the lazier paradigm favoring the theory of everything is more likely to win in the short-term.

This is why it is highly inconvenient that ethical committees might stop objective knowledge.

Without a lazy paradigm of exponential efficiency, the more practical version of efficiency is unlikely to ever succeed.

As people say, the road to hell is paved in good intentions.

With the TOE, perpetual motion could be clearly proven in the ultimate mindset, and it would therefore be built, and humanity could save itself from any practical disaster.

But without a TOE, there would not even be lazy people to defend perpetual motion as the entire theorem would be deemed unfounded, and this might be equivalent to a superstition-infused dark-age where perpetual motion is regarded as demonic.

You can see the importance of the last few pages.

Perpetual motion is an important paradigm, but people seem to think it dangles by an invincible thread.

One of the goals of this book is to make perpetual motion more threatening, and also simultaneously much more technologically appealing.

Perhaps I am dramatizing too much the human survival quandary, but if there is anything practical left to exaggerate it may as well be the peril of the human condition.

Currently all humans are mortal, and anything promising immortality might seem like a very lucky star indeed. Fortunately, the paradigm of perpetual motion, though more-traditionally failed, when combined with higher efficiency could mean something lucky, even if the luck seems to only come in small amounts.

Perhaps over time, humans will build a 'karma elevator' which will save future inventors from the strange obtusity which has plagued our current engineers, in their seeming unwillingness to provide for complete immortality.

It is my belief that improved optimism and economics could go a long way towards un-poisoning the human race, leading to a human equivalent to perpetual motion.

Perpetual motion seems to be the only field where robots currently lead, which makes it seem oddly contemporary.

CHAPTER 7: THE DIFFERENCE BETWEEN MIRACLES AND MIRACLES

The paradigm of perpetual motion is more promising than it initially seems, for a reason that will become obvious.

Spiritual religions traditionally require one thing to prove godhood: performing miracles.

Except miracles were traditionally reserved for those who would engage in some type of sacrifice.

For that reason, perpetual motion poses a two-fold advantage on religion:

(1) It can do something that seems miraculous, i.g. provide free power, and:
(2) It can provide free power without requiring a spiritual sacrifice.

Let me go on about the importance of perpetual motion for miracles:

Self-power is an object of fascination which seems obviously magical.

Imagine, self-mixing bowls or bowls that cause fluids to percolate.

Books that could display dynamic images without even draining batteries.

If these seem miraculous, it is only the beginning.

These devices involve the type of inventions which I already described.

This is a process which is becoming ever-more-real!

Some might consider perpetual motion indistinguishable from magic in the 21st century.

Yet perpetual motion is not spiritually tainted with religious wars like religions are.

CHAPTER 8: THE ADVANTAGES FOR ATHEISM

Though you might now think religious overtones are a problem, black swans are singularly unique.

They pose advantages for Atheism too.

Oh, you didn't consider that?

What happens, Atheists, when miracles are reduced to practicality?

You hadn't considered that, had you?

That is precisely the process where religion is defeated.

It is the moment when all superstition fleets.

It is the triumph of the empirical sciences.

It is the disbandonment of all false belief systems.

It is the approach of the complete, practical existence.

It might even be the end of philosophy.

The beginning of empirical realization.

The end of ignominy.

The end of un-truth and false ideology.

Perpetual motion makes miracles seem normal.

Actually normal! Consider that! It might be hard to grasp!

It could make a scientist feel religious!

CHAPTER 9: NEW SECULARISM

The likely emergence of a post-religious, potentially post-scientific paradigm opens a hole in our idea of secularism.

Science is accustomed to the conquest of superstition, but not at the expense of science.

Likewise, religion is used to dogmatic belief systems, but without reference to repeatable miracles.

What may be called the 'new secularism' follows the trend since the beginning of religious tolerance in America (a relatively non-dogmatic institution) towards improved education and improved living conditions, and could thus be seen as the success of technocracy.

However, it is not just technocracy in the scientific sense, but also in a kind of post-dramatic sense.

The achievement of mechanical practicality is a lofty goal. No one except Archimedes would frown on it.

Likewise, the achievement of a Theory of Anything is also one of the loftiest goals within the abstract domain.

The completion of the abstract and material at a new heightened level allows for the fulfillment of the paradigmatic golden age vibe which the Chinese and the Classical Greeks must have known.

Isolated from history, we wouldn't guess that more than one Golden Age is possible.

And realizing this is a transformation.

However, I have thought that the two halves of the black swans merits a new term:

'DOUBLE GOLDEN AGE': An age which has both mastery of energy and of knowledge.

What is meant by the New Secularism is the secular potential of this new Golden Age concept.

CHAPTER 10: UNIVERSAL COMPUTATION

One of the potentials of research that is the basis for much of the excitement about exponential efficiency is the idea of universal knowledge which led to the Theory of Anything.

Universal--in other words, coherent—knowledge is the theme which initially permits exponential efficiency to occur in the abstract. The way this takes place is similar to perpetual motion.

It was found in my work from 2013 that polar axes need only rotate diagonally, and must be opposed diagonally to reach the furthest possible distance.

The result of this was an efficient permutation in the 2-d, with efficient permutation being a necessary end-goal of the most efficient (at that time at least) conceivable abstract processes.

Connecting the abstract with the material, it was possible to conceive of the general idea of exponential efficiency, and then also the objective nature of black swans.

Taking objective knowledge and perpetual motion as examples, it was possible to extract some core statistics which were allowed to inform the actual Theory of Everything.

CHAPTER 11: A FULLY-REDUCED TOE

By 2022 a fully-reduced TOE was possible which predicted that energy was always subtracted, and that efficiency was a positive modifier.

This theory predicted a very basic similarity between the mathematics for objective knowledge and for perpetual motion.

Taking a modulo number such as three, a difference of -1 for basic abstraction would produce results of 4, the number of items in the set. But adding -1 and 3 would produce 2, the number of deductions.

Similarly, in perpetual motion, a leverage of 3, and a difference of 1 would produce a min results of 2. But adding 1 and 3 would produce the maximum effective leverage which still permits the min.

In this way, both forms of exponential efficiency may be allowed to use identical equations.

Since the two versions of the formula both express black swans, this level of simplification is truly incredible.

CHAPTER 12: TOE PARADIGMS

Needless to say, since 2013 optimism increased, and perhaps more so once the Theory of Anything was finally put into writing in 2019.

The optimism largely concerned the theory of Categorical Deduction (objectivism) because the connection to perpetual motion was largely unknown to anyone else.

Nonetheless, perpetual motion was (whether known or not), an important supporting factor, which by 2020 had inspired the collation of the two arms of the TOE into a general Function Spectrum, which ultimately led to the earlier insights on the mathematics.

As for myself, I continue to hope that the TOE will inspire some amazing computational wonders along the lines of discovering technologies of equal importance to perpetual motion machines.

I deem that this is possible, though I do not know the timeframe.

This insight is one of the reasons that it makes sense that the TOE is of equal or even better importance to perpetual motion, though in my mind this remains a highly radical thesis. Apart from my deep love for coherence theory perpetual motion is obviously more important and interesting.

CHAPTER 13: EXPONENTIAL PARADIGMS

Sometime in the future we can hope to bridge the gap between 1-dimensional economics and the true economics of the future.

Bridging the gap will obviously involve some type of exponent. The nouveau swans are one possible way to do it. In my most general thinking there could be others, but by and large I consider the nouveau swans to be the best possible failsafes imaginable other than immortality or godhood. And added to that, these paradigms might actually lead to immortality if humans survive enough.

There are some obvious applications of perpetual motion once one considers the topic carefully. Some of them are listed on the next page. One of the most inspiring is perhaps the idea of the 'free bank' or 'exponential investment'. In a society which has sufficient technology and its energy needs met, once certain technologies such as 'atomizers' to make food are mass-produced, energy becomes equivalent to a magic power, or at least, a major guarantor of infrastructure. As of this writing, construction cranes apparently don't operate by free energy. I find this disturbing.

On the next page you can find some of the applications of perpetual motion…

A CONTIGUOSLY COHERENT SUMMARY OF PERPETUAL MOTION RESEARCH

perpetual motion —ENERGY— BANKING —INDUSTRY— RESEARCH — MEDICAL—

APPLIED PMMS	BANK TOYS	UNLIMITED ELECTRICITY	IMMORTAL RESEARCH	IMMORT-ALITY
LAND	REAL ESTATE	GRID	AT-SOURCE	QUAL OF LIFE
FLYING	SECURITY	OFF-GRID	OFF-SOURCE	LIFE EXTENSION
WATER	LIQUID	HIGH-POWER	DEDICATED	IMMUNITY
SPACE	STATIC	ASTRONOMIC	LONG-LASTING	PERPETUATION
ELEVATORS	INVESTMENT	EXPONENTIAL	ESCALATIONAL	IMPROVEMENTS
ESCALATORS	CONSUMER	UTILITY	FAILSAFE	CONVENIENCES
APPLIANCES	SERVICES	PORTABLE	STANDALONE	POWERS
MOBILITY	INDUSTRIAL	FLEXIBLE SITE	BAREBONES	RELOCATION
MILITARY	RELIEF	COMPOUNDED	TECH-READY	ADDED DEFENSE
LUXURY	PROSPECTING	PERMANENT	PROPHETIC	CONTINUITY

REPRODUCIBLE UNDER NATHAN LARKIN COPPEDGE

CHAPTER 14: EXPONENTIAL SWANS

On the far reach of what I normally consider there are notions of how to expand the neology to include even greater advancement.

Some of these concepts include hyper-efficiency, meta-efficiency, meta-coherence, and hyperbolic coherence.

One of the more advanced ones is the notion of exponential swans. Though if one were lazy one would simply compound the definitions, I find that inconvenient and I would rather telescope the nouveau swans within the traditional idea of black swans, and use the term 'exponential swans' as a remote and advanced possibility.

Since the nouveau swans are coherent, it is likely that exponential swans must either be a combination of the two principles, or something far more advanced within the range of technical possibility, perhaps some sort of physical knowledge or abstract perpetual motion, like mechanical survival or matchik.

I can predict however, something of what this type of matchik would be like. It would be something like having a knowledge object or readable mathematical characteristics, either of which have, or ideally have, what we might consider magic properties. The invention of exponential swans might be the invention of these properties and perhaps the natural interface.

CHAPTER 15: INTERMEDIATE IDEAS

Somewhere along the path I began to consider how much the nouveau swans anticipate with a high degree of accuracy what seems to be nearly any later invention.

But then I began to turn against this belief, thinking that had I believed that I would have in effect proven that technology had reached its zenith already.

Some concepts such as the magical basin make one believe that when they are made, that civilization is already perfected.

I can anticipate this effect happening, and I think it is part of the good fortune of the matter that because of this historical elongation that occurs, that it is part of the natural process of immortality.

Now THAT I can say, is an INTERMEDIATE IDEA.

It is this type of thinking that leads one to the advanced notion of coherent drugs: that is, drugs which are immaterial, but still beneficial.

After all, if one half of everything is abstract, surely drugs could be abstract too. Everyone can be tricked into thinking that drugs are more than half of everything.

CHAPTER 16: THE PERPETUAL INSTITUTE

If no other immortality arrives, I can imagine founding a perpetual institute. Such an organization would be supported by its influence on the perpetual motion field, and would use its power to perpetuate the economics of perpetual motion.

To me, this is an early idea of immortality. The entity which can claim omniscience and omnipotence of a kind, through the nouveau swans. If it becomes benevolent and omnipresent it would seem to have achieved a kind of godhood, though I suspect this simply translates as good luck, and maybe some technical discoveries.

Still, luck with technical discoveries is what humans currently consider immortal.

Everything about the perpetual institute somehow means immortality. It is a partial integration of the ultimate longevity.

I can imagine that this Institute would lead to further institutes much in the way the Chinese inadvertently founded Western ideology.

At that point I feel that I am connecting with alien intelligence.

CHAPTER 17: REACTIVE MECHANISMS

Before I knew much of what to do with the function spectrum, my mind leapt to a possibility with Difference +5. My immediate thought was that this value, which represented < 500% OU corresponded with some type of chemical development in perpetual motion. There is thought to be some way in which magnets, or perhaps separated compartments of liquid, can interact, using a perhaps newly-discovered mechanical chemistry which adopts some of the properties of perpetual motion.

Perhaps more likely is simply compounding other machines in an efficient way, still ideas such as nano-perpetual motion, antiforces, submarines, amphibious devices, and reactive chemistry obviously have some potential once they are discovered. And the existence of perpetual motion would virtually guarantee that they also have results.

Until more complicated combinations are discovered, I am forced to assume that Difference +5 indeed corresponds with some special development in chemical perpetual motion.

CHAPTER 18: QUANTUM MADNESS

Some thinking which was involved in coherence had me consider topics in physics such as time-travel, biological immortality, and the Many Worlds Hypothesis. I'm not completely against all these theories (and try to found new disciplines where I can) though I tend to be slightly skeptical at first.

One thing that arrived with the idea of coherent drugs was a concomitant idea of the sheer irrationality of madness.

If one thinks about the metaphorical health benefits of natural cures for madness, it is astonishing. It's almost like abstract ambergris.

If one has the imaginative potential, one could propose nominal cures for just about anything and even quickly out-do recent traditions just formulating some new strong type of hypothesis.

This realization and the study of the Coherent Brain contributed to a notion that coherence finally connotes exceeding intelligence, like superintelligence, or alien technology.

The entire neighborhood of concepts related to quantum madness all seem to have a similar very excellent effect.

CHAPTER 19: SUPERCULTURES

One of the major inspirations for my Golden Age Superstrategy diagram was the study of Cultural Superstrategies.

According to this theory, American culture is dominating, but inherited its dominance through an overlapping chain of attributes from the Chinese, who still exist and define the original source logic.

The next development that could occur after the Americans probably extends mass production into perpetual motion, creating a culture of wealth.

If the culture of wealth does not succeed, then America may be the last dominant culture.

However, I have predicted a long series of possible developments even moving in overlapping attributes beyond the Rich Culture. Some of them may involve what seem like improbable magical developments. Since the black swans seem to predict magic, however, the chain of probability becomes more likely.

I now think of the future cultures as the possible inheritance of the TOE.

Though in my current time it is impossible to tell.

CHAPTER 20: INTELLECTUAL TOE

When I discovered the Great Philosophy Historical Model based on an inspiration from an African-American professor, it seemed like too much of a coincidence that the number of ideal ideas was 20, because this seemed to suggest that the TOE25 categories minus the negative dimensions would always equal the number of archetypal ideas.

Since I already knew the TOE represented particularly the first and second 'universe' counting downwards from the upper left square, it made sense that TOEs were a narrow range of the TOE results, and consequently, with the evidence of Modular Ideas, I began to think there were a bevy of constants implicated in the TOE.

With the existence of TOE constants it became possible to predict waveform technologies with perhaps some degree of accuracy.

It is the waveform technologies which seems to suggest a unification of perpetual motion and the TOE could be located within older material sciences, though of course only by adopting extremely esoteric technologies which are still considered far out on the limb of normal physical possibility.

CHAPTER 21: DIVINE NATHAN

I have determined most gods seem to be lacking in credentials. Maybe this is not surprising. But that doesn't mean I have implicated myself.

Nonetheless, there is a method, known as Method-21 which seems to count as godhood.

It is the ability to make a perfect 21-item method.

Though limited by language at times, the method seems to be a fair predictor of some level of supreme significance.

The method has applied to Zheng Guo, who lived long and knew how to fly. And also to Marie Antoinette who founded America and was very rich. And also to Nathan Coppedge who invented the two halves of the Theory of Everything.

Whoever solves method-21 even unconsciously becomes a nominal God unless more than a 25-category TOE is appropriate for them personally.

CHAPTER 22: PARADOXICAL HISTORY

Objective histories can be fascinating, because they show a degree of honesty and transcendence which most ordinary histories lack.

If one considers a history of paradoxes one is likely to consider paradoxical history, which turns out to be a transcendent and divine concept, at least similar to wizard thinking.

Paradoxical history is essentially the world which has 4-dimensional choices, the world of selective complexity or irrational irrationality.

Having conceived of paradoxical paradoxes, the concept of paradoxical history becomes much more interesting, like an architecture of transcendence.

The existence of meaningful concepts turned my mind to the constant 5/32, which encapsulated basic meaning.

Only with a mathematical ground could one hope to transition between these ancient abstract blocks.

I began to wonder about the potential of magic in making the soul immortal in real life.

CHAPTER 23: METABOLISM

It was found four times the perimeter categories in the TOE minus the total categories (TC) equals the digestion number.

This number is thought to lead to human evolution through the series: 39, 47, 39.

The earlier concepts of metabolic metaphysics and meta-metabolism evidently inspired the concept, by predicting that biological immortality was a product of philosophical dimensionism.

Metaphysics is also a traditional route to immortality since the time of Zheng Guo and even as far back as 7,000,000 BC.

CHAPTER 24: SOUL RESEARCH

If there was a better theory than omniscience it might be some kind of diagram, or one might guess at the formula for souls…

At this point I invented the complexity diagram and gave up on diagrams unless they seemed simple to me.

Using a theory from Socrates that the soul was ironic, I formed an attempt to reconstruct the souls of books at Alexandria…

Title: [Quality of X] [Opp Qualifier]

Soul: If you [X] [Qualifier] natural result [Opp X Clarified]

It was later theorized although originally it was a classical attempt, it might be used for modern research.

CHAPTER 25: TO DABBLE WITH DISTANCE

I had a moment with perpetual motion where I had a sensation of 'crossing the last barrier'. Otherwise, one is convinced that one must defeat angels.

Theories of distance have become important for me, since I was 5-years-old and saw dust settling on a plane of glass, which I had a unique feeling about and called 'the dimensional plane'.

Much later I developed the concept of the 'Elidian Leap' which was a pseudo-occult idea of traveling through genius.

Then I thought of the Gambit of Ambition which applied a similar concept to golden ages. If one age like black swans was fulfilled one could then ratchet up the criteria and it would help predict the next most ambitious quest.

Sometimes I thought of my involvement in Hyper-Cubism as an experimentation in logic.

CHAPTER 26: DIVINE MOTION MACHINE

There is a tendency to worship perpetual motion.

Not because of Nathan, because it has the attributes of God. It has been shown several times that perpetual motion has divine attributes.

More than representing God himself, perpetual motion aims to run on its own and be beneficial even with no obvious agency.

It makes one wonder if there is some truth to the phrase, 'God from the machine'.

If the machines are what people hopefully claim they are, then they do indeed have benefits which transcend what is traditionally considered average.

The mere existence of perpetual motion machines could start a religion, or a 1000-year party.

Opposing perpetual motion once it starts is unlucky like uttering a curse.

CHAPTER 27: LANGUAGE OF EVERYTHING

A few years into the process I began to realize there were some things missing from human concepts which might help build bigger brains.

One of these was the idea that once you have minute little tools that are quite cool, you may as well make a whole language out of them. It is only from this kind of height that one can perceive that the Function Spectrum lacks content.

From this and the Sublime Constants emerged a project known as the Technological Words of Power. This was an organization of the TOE designed to grant greater detail on its technological properties.

The words of power was an early example of a language of everything.

There was also a dimensional theory of language based on mathematics, and a unified theory of language which predicted that what does not speak one language always speaks another, like a linguistic theory of consciousness.

For the most part the sublime constants seemed more integrated with the TOE, though the Words of Power seemed like the perfect classification system.

CHAPTER 28: DIVINE SWANS

Deeply into this process, I began to see the possible reality, that seeking immortality was the ultimate quest unless it had been lost to time.

And I remembered once when I invented the calendar in Sumeria I may have indeed lost immortality to just such an entity. He had suggested that originality was everywhere and obiquitous, why would I trifle over such a little matter. He insinuated that I was crazy.

This led years later to the concept of Divine Swans: that elevating something to the status of immortality could miraculously solve any problem, including what some consider impossible.

Though I have not investigated it much, it seems to represent the far reaches of swan theory.

CHAPTER 29: DEVILISH SWANS

Once I had the sensation of inventing devilish swans.

And I saw a fantastic scene, and had an odd sensation that the swans were more important than anything and somehow causing reality to wither away, while they absorbed all it's beauty.

From this idea I get the notion that aesthetics could win by fiat even with things like the Theory of Anything, though it seems to require breaking some rules or learning magic.

I'm still thankful I saw the swans though it seems unfair that they were stealing my reality.

I think around then I thought of greatness theory: that everyone achieves no more than one point in Wealth, Popularity, and Originality, with a maximum of 2.5 points.

The point I guess with the swans is that things can always be more real so one cannot really trust anything permanently, there might be trump coming at any moment.

CHAPTER 30: HYPER-SOULS

The fully-reduced TOE theory, later thought to represent golden ages rather than being the most accurate, which negates the difference and adds it to the efficiency led naturally to a theory of hyper-souls, which always have a result of '4' (in fact all souls do).

After this result it was later determined that a formula better than the one derived from Socrates might be nearly impossible to find at least before 2022 CE.

However, it still seems possible that there may be a concept of the hyper-soul, lurking somewhere, though it is thought to involve efficiency which is not above six.

THE BLACK SWAN MARKET, NATHAN COPPEDGE

,,,

THE NEW SCIENCE MANIFESTO

1 HOW DO I MAKE A COUNTRY THAT STAYS ETERNALLY?

Basically, you have to study pre-existing superstrategies.

The superstrategy method is built into the human genome back to the dinosaurs.

The dinosaurs had one strategy, which involved something like 1. Something good, 2. Something bad.

After the dinosaurs everything had something bad, plus the next thing.

In the case of humans, we decided to diversify and have more than one culture of strategy.

However, this resulted in a progressive system where each one replaces the last. I don't mean that the previous cultures are dead necessarily, but they usually don't remain superpowers.

Any culture related to a previous superpower usually won't succeed without founding its own new organizational structure, kind of like ants or beavers.

Because the Russians were part Mongol or use Mongol land, and the Mongols became mostly Chinese, the Russians are unlikely to be a dominant superpower unless the Chinese take over again.

If the Chinese take over again, humanity might die without the Phoenicians or the Chinese might have to split into two different races. Genetics says that probably won't happen because of the need for genetic diversity (maybe that's American propaganda, but I don't know, I don't hear of a lot of innovating in China maybe it's just because I'm not part of the culture).

Cyborgs probably aren't an option because cyborgs ultimate oppose genetics and with it evolution. So Musk will probably not be leading a successful race by himself.

Here is a diagram illustrating. Maybe this is too idealistic, still it is interesting:

Here is a possible conspectus:

Say you look at the superstrategies from the last 12,000 years (the last human age).

THE BLACK SWAN MARKET, NATHAN COPPEDGE

CULTURAL SUPERSTRATEGIES:

Chinese :
* Martialing the arts.
* Overwhelming forces.

Phoenicians :
* Overwhelming forces.
* Religious traditions.

Egyptians :
* Religious traditions.
* Appealing culture.

Greeks :
* Appealing culture.
* Enslaving others' cultures.

Romans :
* Enslaving others' cultures.
* Consolidating power.

French :
* Consolidating power.
* Robbing the people.

British :
* Robbing the people.
* Industrialization.

Americans :
* Industrialization.
* Mass production.

Rich culture:
* Mass production
* Perpetual motion

Sexy culture?
* Perpetual motion?
* Potent orgasm?

The French had weights and measures. The British had empirical philosophy and naval ballistics. The Americans have scientific research such as nuclear energy, semiconductors, and materials science.

Before that, the Romans had engineering. The Greeks had philosophy of science. And the Egyptians had construction.

Although all of the last six supercultures had science, only the recent superculture is what we really call science.

Will this trend continue? Well, it will continue if there's a new science.

2 A PLATINUM CALF ANSWER TO "WHY ARE BAD THINGS STILL HAPPENING IN 2024?"

It's a complex question, and I don't want to be dismissed out of hand.

Maybe Nathan adapted.

- But maybe Nathan had to survive in Venezuela when he was three years old due to his Dad's graduate work. In many worlds maybe Nathan's dead but maybe Nathan is a time-traveler

Maybe actors and rich people adapted.

- But possibly they were circumcised and got male syphilis or gave birth to a child. Or possibly they're gay or really evil or a different species. Maybe rich people have old world problems, but maybe they know about science.

Maybe prostitutes adapted.

- However they are often abused or have many abortions. Maybe they complain a lot, but maybe they reproduce.

Maybe survivalists adapted.

- However, there is limited usefulness for their skills in the modern world. They could get in trouble or run out of money. Maybe they are dangerous, but sometimes they are early adapters.

Maybe immigrants adapted.

- They face a risky situation where the laws might turn against them. Once they're American they might become ordinary consumers with no connection to their earlier country. Immigrants are in bad shape, on the other hand they may bring needed optimism.

If we consider what society might accomplish, it is not 100% clear that science is the big picture. Some of the major factors are marketing, popular trends, the post-Millenium conservatism, and at a stretch new discoveries which are not likely to adopt the same scientific dogma. Remember, when technical shifts occur they are big. New trends are always radical. Otherwise we risk returning to a Medieval worldview.

Inventions like writing and the airplane were radical.

Classification of Black Swans.

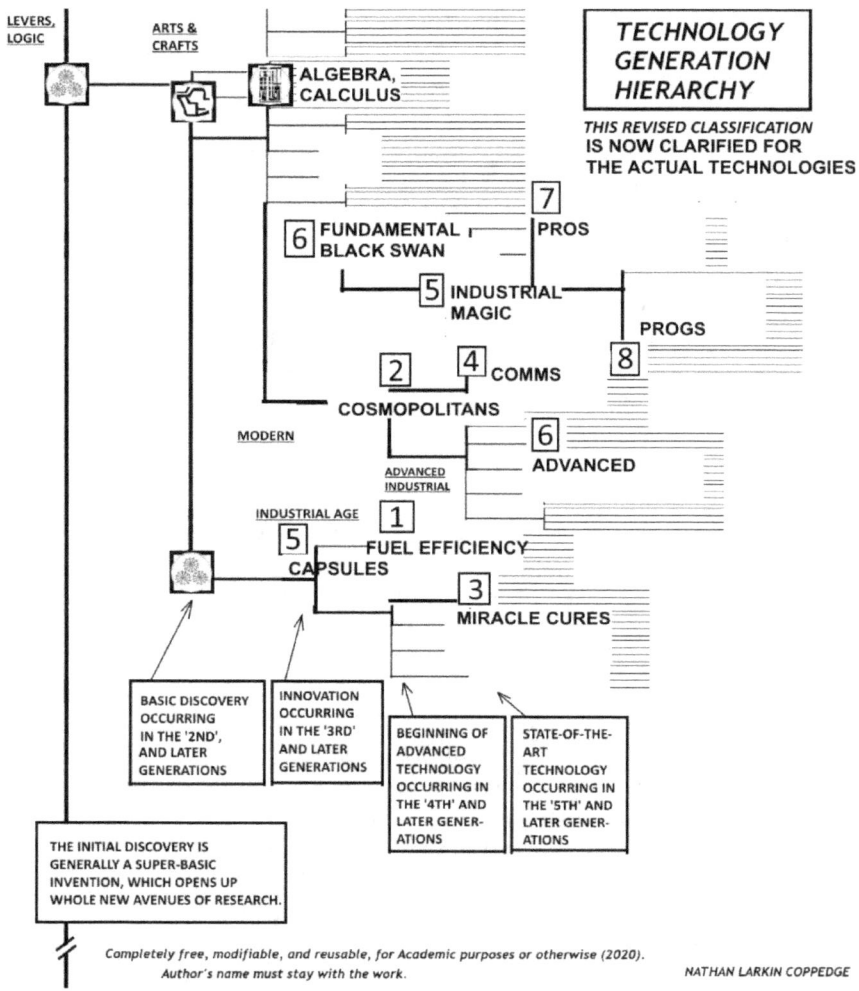

In the above diagram, science takes us to 1.2 and 2.0, and 3.0 and 3.1, but it may get stuck on 3.2, 2.1, 2.2, and 1.2B.

I can surmise firsthand that 3.2 is probably Guo's immortality t-shirt, 2.1 is probably the discovery of linear graph everything and perfect constants using the Theory of Everything and the discovery that what we call the 3rd dimension is really the 4th dimension correlated with 4 max results in the ToE. 1.2B is most likely a very late perpetual motion.

These factors may be important for human survival, but they depend on philosophy. They depend on science only indirectly.

3 PARSING COMPUTERS: "HOW CAN I SHARE AN INVENTION IDEA WITH ELECTRONIC COMPANIES WITHOUT IT BEING STOLEN?"

There was an invention period leading up to 2014 when it may have been possible to exaggerate the importance of a computer for example, and make it look extremely flashy.

However, the advent of app-based performance around 2014 - 2016 privileged certain platforms like 'apple' and 'google'. This meant that the traditional business model was over.

By 2021 this trend against real businesses continued with the advent of COVID-19. People were wearing masks in public. While it might be possible to sell the best video games, I commented, it might not be possible to sell even the best video games profitably anymore. Instead, traditional business models were converted into private- or government- subsidy models, with traditional performance being reduced to a mere bargaining chip for federal or private funds, with smaller players being simply 'recipients' rather than 'donors', a very clear distinction which divides what might be called 'what is left of society', i.e. ordinary people, which could be almost anyone (the 'consumers' and 'immigrants'), and people with resources (which could be almost no one).

In 2013 there was a hidden shift towards privileging Federal performance, where it was possible to break laws and utilize 'deep resources' to create for example, improved combat drones, and government-secure supercomputers. This trend depended unpredictably on developments in quantum computing which weren't precisely quantum. It was a particular logic called Exponential Efficiency developed by Nathan Coppedge on February 2, 2013 which would allow something similar to omniscience using almost zero data. Though the applications were drawn out and even largely ignored at first by the government and even by research agencies like MIT and quantum computing labs, by 2018 or so significant developments existed which showed some hidden possibilities. While these possibilities are underdeveloped, and Coppedge developed some further logics beginning in 2016—still it was nonetheless the beginning of a new paradigm, or at least a paradigm which began to exist at some point. Some made claims they thought were radical that Nietzsche had the same logic, or Immanuel Kant. Still, there was damning evidence that the term 'exponential efficiency' as it existed in 2000 in quantum computing research, simply meant an upward curve, and the term did not even exist before that, or not very publicly.

Nathan Coppedge, who had invented the omniscience idea, also had another idea. In the early-to-mid 2020s he conceived of a set of equations which would show how to create any technology which had a similar efficiency to the omniscience formula. These 'exponentially-efficient technologies' were still theoretical, but the evidence, when it was shown, never seemed to prove them wrong. One of the equations for example, indicated combining simple machines could produce higher efficiencies which were exponentially-efficient just like the omniscience. The math was compatible with use of two-variables on the evidence that adding 100% energy for weightlessness would make a perpetual motion machine which needed +2 difference, which was mathematically compatible with flying machines. Elaborating the equations produced a table of constants which seemed to describe all the major properties of what we would call clever technology.

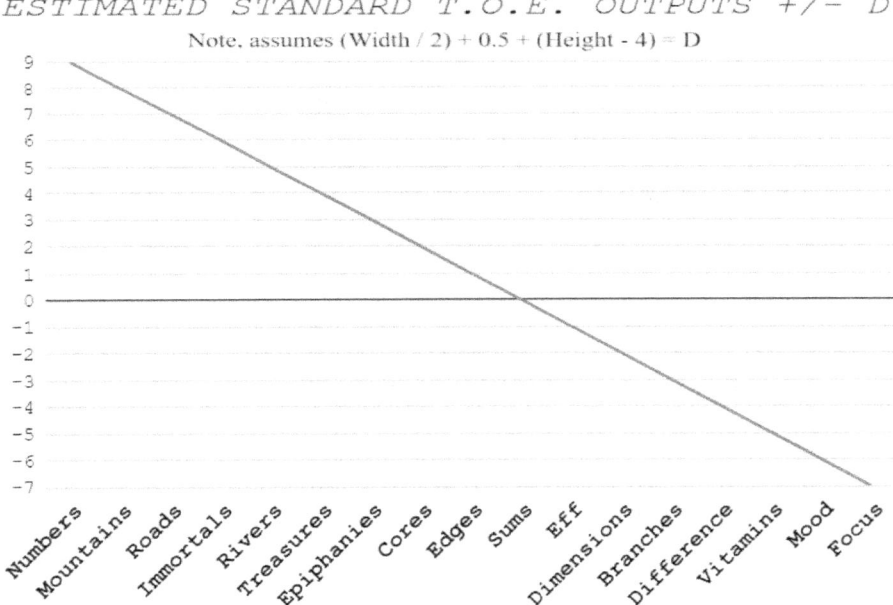

A major point was Nathan's data was publicly released. Without any way of running a company, Nathan was forced to bargain for fame instead of seeking profit.

Using this chart and earlier data helped clarify that Immortality was correlated with Results of 4, and Results of 4 meant four-dimensional. This suggested that wherever perceptual dimensions is two is the same place where Vitamins of -1 appears, which is where what we call immortal technology might first appear, as the barest requirement is the existence of 'ghosts' or 'abstractions'. Traditions like the belief in God depend on the fundamental belief in 'ghosts'. Thus, I had hit on something deep. Since God harked back to Zheng Guo's invention of immortality, most likely I could correlate a vitamins of -1 with the existence of immortality. Maybe not everyone would want to be immortal, but this was a tentative mathematical proof of the possibility of human longevity. Note that if something could trump immortality it could still cause humans to die every time, and would also possibly make every species extinct including humans.

4 POLITICAL INSTABILITY

Had there been a year when America would fall it would have been 2023. So most likely the Chinese will not really take over at this point.

However, it is possible that there is a shift towards a new culture favoring the global rich.

Another point is that in 2023 in my best assessment the top idea was a choice between two new technologies:

- Reduced firearm recoil, and:
- Biological immortality.

If biological immortality never has a best year (that is, probably if its best year is not 2023, but not necessarily), then it is possible all species in the universe will die.

On the other hand, reduced firearm recoil sounds more American.

This may suggest either a shift towards immortality and survival, or a shift towards superficial survival and warlordism. However, this is somewhat suspicious because the very concept of having a best idea of the year is much smarter than warlordism as a social concept, which piggybacks us to the idea that since intelligent social concepts are intelligent, most likely the idea from 2023 is intelligent. However, clearly enough OU Recoil would be seen at least by females as unintelligent.

However, if OU Recoil is unintelligent, the only top idea for 2023 seems to be immortality.

If no best idea occurs in 2023, this would suggest a slip into dark agism which could be even lower level than warlordism, with warlordism already refuted, suggesting that dark agism is already refuted too.

5 SOME PEOPLE WANT TO REMAIN IN THE 20TH CENTURY

Strategic question.

You can't really. History progresses.

However, you can support the latest inventions to prevent a serious backslide into radicalism or dark agery.

Remember it's somewhat relative. Even inventions from the 70s or later might be considered 'dark age' now. It's not because they were better inventions. It's because history must progress or its a sign of wasting time and wasting the human brain.

6 INITIATION INTO PROGRESSIVE TECHNOLOGY

As soon as younger people realize that AI can make psychic-level predictions about things like technology they will turn towards supporting new ideas, at which point something like either:

- A new interface. Or,
- A non-interface technology…

Will become necessary. However, the shift towards new technology suggests what will be adopted is not a previously recognized technology concept. The pressure is on to think of something other than quantum computers, tokamaks, electric cars, and traditional green energy.

…

NOTES:

- Predictions: In eighty-one years we can usually expect an iteration of this year's idea. However, this is mainly true beginning in 1992.

…

THE GREAT COPERNICAN DIAGRAM BY COPPEDGE (2022) [A1]

THE BLACK SWAN MARKET, NATHAN COPPEDGE

	TECH COMPLEX	TECH SIMPLE	ARTISTIC SIMPLE	ARTISTIC COMPLEX	COSM COMPLEX	COSM SIMPLE	PHYSICAL SIMPLE	PHYSICAL COMPLEX	NEW INVENTION
TECH COMPLEX	1. 1200s, 2050 TECH COMPLEX TECH COMPLEX Machines	2. 10 1300s, 1830s40s TECH SIMPLE TECH COMPLEX Incindiaries Photog	3. 19 1400s, 1950s ARTISTIC SIMPLE TECH COMPLEX Ikons Computers	4. 28 1500s, 1996 ART COMPLEX TECH COMPLEX Landscape From Parts Unknown	5. 37 1600s, 2005 COSM COMPLEX TECH COMPLEX Calc Rapid Pace	6. 46 1700-49, 2014 COSM SIMPLE TECH COMPLEX Truthie Blockchain	7. 55 1750-99, 2023 PHYSICAL SIMPLE TECH COMPLEX America BioImmort	8. 64 1800-10, 2032 PHYS COMPLEX TECH COMPLEX Locomotion	9. 73 1810s, 20, 2041 NEW INVENTION TECH COMPLEX CapitalGains
TECH SIMPLE		11. 1850s 1860s TECH SIMPLE TECH SIMPLE Real mcCoy	12. 20 1870 1880 50s 60s ARTISTIC SIMPLE TECH SIMPLE Modernism Robots	13. 29 1890s 00 1997 ART COMPLEX TECH SIMPLE Head to Head	14. 38 1900s, 2006 COSM COMPLEX TECH SIMPLE Generalism Perpetual Motion	15. 47 1910s,, 2015 COSM SIMPLE TECH SIMPLE Specialism Magic Angle	16. 56 1920s 2024 PHYSICAL SIMPLE TECH SIMPLE Relativism	17. 65 20s, 30s, 2033 PHYS COMPLEX TECH SIMPLE Relativity	18. 74 40s, 50s, 2042 NEW INVENTION TECH SIMPLE Nukes
ART SIMPLE			21. 1960s ARTISTIC SIMPLE ARTISTIC SIMPLE ColorPhotos	22. 30 1970s, 1998 ART COMPLEX ART SIMPLE MCEscherDigitalAge	23. 39 1980s, 2007 COSM COMPLEX ART SIMPLE Extraterrestrials Photo-Realism	24. 48 1992, 2016 COSM SIMPLE ART SIMPLE EncinoMan ClearCutArt	25. 57 1993, 2025 PHYSICAL SIMPLE ART SIMPLE FastComputers	26. 66 1994, 2034 PHYS COMPLEX ART SIMPLE Crack Fiends	27. 75 1995, 2043 NEW INVENTION ART SIMPLE Singularity
ART COMPLEX				31. 1999 ART COMPLEX ART COMPLEX High Graphics	32. 40 2000, 2008 COSM COMPLEX ART COMPLEX Greenhouseeffect Hyper-Cubism	33. 49 2001, 2017 COSM SIMPLE ART COMPLEX Artificial Reality Fantasy Art	34. 58 2002, 2026 PHYSICAL SIMPLE ART COMPLEX AstroidImpacts	35. 67 2003, 2035 PHYS COMPLEX ART COMPLEX Moore'sLaw	36. 76 2004, 2044 NEW INVENTION ART COMPLEX Coherence
COSM COMPLEX					41 TrnMetaph2009 COSM COMPLEX COSM COMPLEX	42. 50 2010, 2018 COSM SIMPLE COSM COMPLEX HoloUnivDisintegral	43. 59 2011, 2027 PHYSICAL SIMPLE COSM COMPLEX Sublimsm	44. 68 2012, 2036 PHYS COMPLEX COSM COMPLEX Higgs	45. 77 2013, 2045 NEW INVENTION COSM COMPLEX ExpEff
COSM SIMPLE						51 TOE, 2019 COSM SIMPLE COSM SIMPLE	52. 60 2020, 2028 PHYSICAL SIMPLE COSM SIMPLE FunSpec	53. 69 2021, 2037 PHYS COMPLEX COSM SIMPLE DimLang	54. 78 2022, 2046 NEW INVENTION COSM SIMPLE Meaningful Constants
PHYS SIMPLE							61. 2029 PHYSICAL SIMPLE PHYSICAL SIMPLE	62. 70 2030, 2038 PHYS COMPLEX PHYSICAL SIMPLE	63. 79 2031, 2047 NEW INVENTION PHYSICAL SIMPLE
PHYS COMPLEX								71. 2039 PHYS COMPLEX PHYS COMPLEX	72. 80 2040, 2048 NEW INVENTION PHYS COMPLEX
NEW INVENTION									81. 2049 NEW INVENTION NEW INVENTION

REPRODUCIBLE UNDER NATHAN COPPEDGE

PROGRESS IN TRADITIONAL SCIENCE IS STILL POSSIBLE, TOO

- The Chemical Puzzle Just Became Clearer.

THE BLACK SWAN MARKET, NATHAN COPPEDGE

BOOK RECOMMENDATIONS
THE BOOK OF THE FOUR

THE PHENOMENAL HISTORY

THE NECESSARY PERFECTIONS

THE BLACK SWAN MARKET

100 GREAT PERPETUAL MOTION MACHINES

50 GREAT FLYING AND UNDERWATER PERPETUAL MOTION MACHINES

THE HISTORY OF COHERENCE

THE HISTORY OF PERPETUAL MOTION MACHINES

NECESSARY SYSTEMS

SCIENTIFIC THEORIES

THE ALCHEMY

THE SYSTEM OF ALL SYSTEMS

Bio

Nathan Coppedge (b.1982), is a philosopher, artist, inventor, poet, and member of the international honor society for philosophers. A prolific author with over 200 books published on Amazon, he is a perpetual motioneer, famous quotable, and internationally-selling Hyper-Cubist. A one-time member of Tesla Society UK online and PESWiki, and founder of many Facebook groups, he lives near Yale University.

www.ingramcontent.com/pod-product-compliance
Lightning Source LLC
Chambersburg PA
CBHW071121240526
45465CB00022B/736